ESSENTIAL
MANAGERS
PRESENTING

ESSENTIAL
MANAGERS
PRESENTING

Penguin
Random
House

Written by Aileen Pincus

Senior Art Editor Gillian Andrews
Project Editor Hugo Wilkinson
Designer XAB Design
Editor Louise Tucker
UK Editor Sam Kennedy
US Editors Margaret Parrish, Jill Hamilton
Managing Editor Stephanie Farrow
Senior Managing Art Editor Lee Griffiths
Production Editor Nikoleta Parasaki
Production Controller Mandy Inness
Jacket Designer Mark Cavanagh
Design Development Manager Sophia M.T.T.

DK Delhi
Senior Art Editor Govind Mittal
Art Editor Vikas Chauhan
DTP Designer Vishal Bhatia

First American Edition, 2008
This American Edition, 2015

Published in the United States by
DK Publishing
345 Hudson Street
New York, New York 10014

A Penguin Random House Company

15 16 17 18 19 10 9 8 7 6 5 4 3 2 1

001-275337-May/2015

Published in Great Britain by
Dorling Kindersley Limited.

A catalog record for this book is available from the
Library of Congress.

ISBN 978-1-4654-3415-9

DK books are available at special discounts when
purchased in bulk for sales promotions, premiums,
fund-raising, or educational use. For details, contact:
DK Publishing Special Markets, 345 Hudson Street,
New York, New York 10014 or SpecialSales@dk.com.

Color reproduction by Colourscan, Singapore
Printed in China

www.dk.com

Contents

Introduction

The increasing pace and competitiveness of business make the need for communication all the more urgent. It is not surprising that presentations have become an essential tool for business communication in workplaces around the world. After all, ideas need to be shared in a clear and convincing way if they are to influence others.

Every presentation is a pitch in which you must sell your ideas to colleagues or outside audiences. This holds true whether your intention is to inform or to persuade, whether you are delivering a formal speech from behind a podium, a presentation using visual aids, an informal address to your staff, or a briefing distributed through the media.

Successful presenters understand what they must communicate, who they are communicating with, and for what reason. With preparation and practice—and working through each of these elements—anyone can learn to plan, assemble, and deliver a successful presentation every time.

The elements of great presentations are described in this guide in practical detail, making it ideal for new managers and experienced communicators alike.

Planning to **present**

A presentation is a way of informing, inspiring, and motivating other people. Whether your audience is a group of receptive colleagues, demanding clients, or strict regulators, your job is to influence the way they think and feel about your message. No matter how charismatic you may be, success depends on careful planning of your content and delivery.

01

Putting the audience first

Presenting successfully means stepping back from your own knowledge of your subject. Examine what you want to say and how you convey that information from the perspective of the audience. Their priorities will almost always be different from yours.

Identifying the need

A presentation serves a very different purpose from a written report—it is far more than just another vehicle for information. A presentation allows an audience to gain knowledge by watching, listening, and being inspired by you. Audiences come not to learn everything you know about a subject but to gain your perspective—they are likely to remember only the big themes even a short time afterward. Good presenters understand that audiences are looking for information in context, not in full detail, so ask yourself what you can add through your presentation of the subject.

> **Audiences** are likely to **remember** only the **big themes** even a short time afterward

Tip

MIND YOUR LANGUAGE
Check the **language abilities** of your **audience**—if you do not share the same first language, you will need to make allowances.

Researching the audience

Get to know your audience, even before you plan your presentation. Talk to the organizer of the event about their expectations, and if possible, engage with those attending ahead of time; ask them about their existing level of knowledge, and what they hope to hear about. Work out if they need persuading, informing, educating, motivating, or a mixture of all these. The more you understand your audience's expectations, the better you'll be able to meet them.

ASK YOURSELF...
Who is my audience?   **YES   NO**

1 Do I know who will be **listening**...☐   ☐

2 Do I know how much they already know? Is there a **common understanding** to build on?...☐   ☐

3 Do I know their **expectations?** Will they hold any **preconceived notions** about the subject?.....................................☐   ☐

4 Do I know what I want them to **learn?** What do I expect them to do with that **knowledge?**...☐   ☐

5 Do I know what I will say to **accomplish my goals?**.....................☐   ☐

Focusing your message
Identify the essential information you want your audience to understand and remember—no more than three such core messages. Build your presentation around these points and add supporting details where necessary—but remember that less is more when it comes to presentation. Make your key points emphatically and repeatedly and don't try to be too subtle or clever. Look for the overlap between what you want to say and what your audience wants to hear.

Tip

MATCH THINKING STYLES
Is your audience made up of **creative** thinkers or analysts? Bear in mind that you'll need to tailor your **presentation** content and your **delivery** to match their thinking style.

Presenting and selling

Presentations serve a variety of purposes. They can be used to inspire and motivate people or they can be designed to convey information formally (as in a lecture) or informally (as in a team briefing). But most often, they are used to promote a product, service, or idea, or to persuade stakeholders about a particular course of action. In other words—whether overtly or covertly—most presentations aim to sell.

Pitching your ideas

The better you can meet the needs of your audience, the more successful your presentation will be. So when selling anything, from an idea to a product, your presentation should focus on how it will help your audience, how it will solve their problems. Whenever you talk about your idea, product, or service, don't just list its features—express them as benefits.

Throughout your presentation, your audience will be constantly assessing both your trustworthiness and the strength of your "sell." You need to be able to "read" their reactions so that you can address their concerns. Successful presenters do this by inviting many questions from the audience and encouraging them to interrupt; the questions and comments from the audience provide vital feedback.

> Your presentation should **focus on** how it will **help your audience**

Selling successfully in your presentation

SELL BENEFITS, NOT FEATURES

The presentation must center on **what matters most** to the buyer—general discussion won't do. Talk about **specific benefits.** How does the product or service help to solve a problem or improve a situation?

BELIEVE WHAT YOU ARE SAYING

An **animated, enthusiastic** presentation is a must. Buyers do not want to buy from someone who doesn't appear **fully committed** to the product, even if it is relevant to their needs.

EXPECT TO CLOSE

If the presentation is **effective,** the decision to buy, or buy in, is a natural next step. Be prepared to ask for some kind of **commitment** and agree to take **immediate action,** even if it is only setting up another meeting.

SHOW, DON'T TELL

Visual representations and physical demonstrations bring sales presentations to life. People **remember** what they **see and do** for themselves, so be **creative.**

KNOW YOUR STUFF

To establish your **credibility,** you need to know a great deal about your product or service. As well as handling general, predictable questions, be prepared to demonstrate your **knowledge in every respect**.

In focus

THE TWO-MINUTE PRESENTATION

We often encounter people casually— between meetings or in quick conversations at conferences. It pays to develop a focused two-minute pitch that introduces you, your business, and the unique value you can offer. The pitch should be very easy to understand, describe the solutions you offer, and reflect your passion about what you do. A good two-minute pitch will get you a surprising number of follow-up meetings.

Tip

GET TO THE POINT
Engage your audience by addressing what they want to know as quickly as possible. Avoid **opening** your presentation with background about you or your company—when it was founded, where it's located, etc.

Presenting formally

In many presentations, you are in control of what you say and how you say it. But be aware that some types of presentation are much more formal, following rules, requirements, timescales, or formats dictated by the audience or by a third party. They include presentations to boards, regulatory bodies, and examination and assessment panels, all of which require high levels of planning and rigorous attention to detail.

Keeping focused

When you are asked to make a formal presentation, always request guidance about what is expected from you—what is the desired length, content, and context of your material. Play it safe—don't attempt to be too innovative with the structure; rather, stick with a tried and tested formula.

Introduce the topic, the argument you are about to make, and the conclusion that you will reach.

How to structure a formal presentation

Preparing to succeed

Before a formal presentation, seek out people who know the members of the board. Find out everything you can about their backgrounds, concerns, and predispositions. Use what you have learned to prepare your arguments carefully; if appropriate, try to gain advance support for your position with members of the board.

Confidence is another key success factor. You will be expected to take a strong stand and support all your arguments with compelling evidence. Handle challenges with calm assurance and keep in mind that it is your position, rather than your personality, that is under attack. Finally, if you are presenting with colleagues, make sure you "get your story straight"—that all your materials are consistent.

Presenting to a board

Keep your presentation concise and limit the detail that you include. If presenting to a board of directors, for example, bear in mind that they don't get involved in day-to-day management and have many demands on their time. Focus on what they really need to know, but ensure you don't withhold anything important—choose your words very carefully to ensure that you cannot be interpreted as being misleading.

Being a panelist

Panel presentations are often a feature of conferences. If you are asked to be a panelist, make sure you understand the specific areas or questions you have been invited to address. Find out who is talking before and after you, and what they are focusing on to avoid repeating their content.

Build flexibility into your presentation, since time slots often shift to accommodate delays. Make sure you have time to present your key points. If you feel the topic is too complex for the time frame, suggest an alternative.

You will be expected to **take a strong stand** and support it with **compelling evidence**

Following protocol

Some expert panels are very formally structured, with individual members asked to stand and present on a topic in turn before fielding questions from other panelists or the audience. Others are much looser, with any panelist permitted to interject, or add remarks or questions at any time. If the format of your panel is unstructured, always be attentive while others are speaking, don't interrupt others too often, and don't speak for too long. No matter how informal the structure, always take the time to develop your key messages in advance.

Develop your arguments clearly and persuasively, justifying what you say.

Make a conclusion: summarize your main arguments and explain the relevance of the conclusion made; explain why you are confident of your conclusion.

Tip

EXPECT TOUGH QUESTIONS
Formal presentations to boards and panels may be met with adversarial questions—boards may view harsh questioning as perfectly acceptable, so come **prepared** with **robust answers.**

Facilitate discussion of your presentation; check that everyone has understood exactly how you have arrived at your conclusion.

Planning the structure

There are many ways to organize your ideas to create an effective and convincing presentation. Sometimes, the content you need to convey will fall more naturally into one type of structure rather than another. There may also be an element of personal preference—you may simply feel more comfortable with one type of structure than another. But however you choose to organize, the end result must achieve your communication goal. In other words, content always dictates form, not vice versa.

Setting out the basics

All presentation structures share three high-level elements: the introduction or opening, the body or main content, and the conclusion or close. Most of your time will be spent delivering the body, but don't underestimate the importance of opening with an introduction that captures the audience's attention, and tying everything together at the close.

Quick and easy storyboarding

Sticky notes are a useful tool when storyboarding your presentation. Use a different colored note for each type of element: for example, blue for a key message, pink for each proof point that backs up a message, and orange for a visual aid. Reposition the notes to experiment with running order, the balance between "showing" and "telling," and to identify weak sections. Storyboarding is a method of sequencing your ideas that can help you decide how to represent them in a logical and compelling order when planning your presentation. It adds a physical dimension that is especially useful for organizing and understanding the impact of a presentation using visual aids.

75%

of the presentation should be content, **10%** should be **introduction,** and **15%** should be **conclusion**

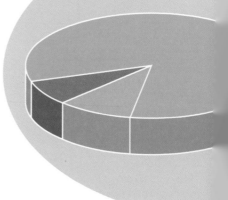

THE INTRODUCTION
Think of your opening as a promise to the audience. It should tell them what they are going to hear, and **why it is important.** This section needs to get their **attention** and give them a reason to keep **listening.**

THE BODY
This is where you **deliver on the promise** you made in your introduction. Here you deliver the facts, analysis, explanation, and comment to fill out your message. **Sustain interest** by keeping the opening promise in mind, and making sure every element advances that **goal.**

THE CONCLUSION
Your close is the "so what?" of your presentation. Remind the audience of your **key points** and clearly articulate where they lead, or conclusions that can be drawn. An effective close demonstrates your **conviction** about the action you are suggesting or the position you hold. While you should spend no more than **15 percent** of your presentation time on the close, remember that it will probably be the section that your audience remembers most clearly after you have finished. Whatever you want them to remember, say it now.

Tip

KEEP IT BALANCED
Your structured content should fall roughly into these proportions: **10 percent** introduction, **75 percent** body, and **15 percent** conclusion. Let each section fulfill its function: don't overload the introduction or bring in new ideas in the conclusion.

Selecting a framework

To structure your presentation for maximum impact, choose a framework sympathetic to its content. For example, if your material is data-driven, use a numbered list; if you are selling a concept, employ case studies. Described here is a selection of useful structural alternatives.

189%

is the estimated increase in audience **retention** of information when irrelevent **pictures and words** are deleted

NUMBERED LIST

Use this model to present **modular information** such as the top competitors in your market. Often **quantitative information** helps your audience to understand the relationship between a list of the items.

1 / 2

PROBLEMS AND SOLUTIONS

Outline a problem, then reveal how to **fix it.** This structure is excellent when discussing change. It can **help** to position you as someone who can **read a situation** clearly, **explain it,** and offer **a way to move forward.**

FEATURES AND BENEFITS

Work through the **elements** of a product or proposal and explain the **positive outcomes** each one can generate. This method works well for more **persuasive sales presentations.**

DEDUCTIVE OR INDUCTIVE?

Deductive reasoning moves from general principles to the specifics ("our market is growing, we should do well"); **inductive reasoning** moves from specifics to **principles** ("we've **done well,** our market is growing").

3 4

Apple was rated the **top brand** for telling the most compelling **story** to their **customers**

MESSAGING

Tell them you are **going to tell** them, **tell them,** and then **tell them you have told them.** This simple structure **works well** provided the messages are clear and backed up with proof.

STORIES AND CASE STUDIES

Present your idea or **argument through a good narrative.** People love **hearing stories,** making this a compelling and forceful presentation method. Keep your story simple and explain the "moral."

COMPARE AND CONTRAST

Put your material **in context** by comparing it with something else. Ensure that similarities and differences **are clear**.

OPTIONS AND OUTCOMES

List some choices and the **pros and cons** of each. Make sure the options are different, not refinements of one idea. If you are going to suggest the best way forward, be prepared to **back it up** with data.

8

TIMELINE

A **chronological structure** is useful for showing **progressive** developments. Its linear structure is intuitive and easy to understand. To avoid seeming one-dimensional, ensure your material has both **purpose and pace**.

9

Opening and closing

Two simple observations of human interaction will help you plan a powerful presentation. First, you only have one chance to make a first impression; and second, people remember longest what they hear last. These observations suggest that the opening and closing parts of your presentation have particular importance. It pays to practice getting these moments right—making them clear, powerful, and engaging.

Opening powerfully

The opening to your presentation serves many functions: it grabs the attention of your audience, establishes your credibility, and sets the stage for what is to come. Don't begin with an extended introduction, lengthy thanks to your hosts, or a recitation of the agenda—you may not be able to engage your audience after such a slow start. Instead, explain to your audience how listening to you will be of benefit to them, and through your confidence, let them see your competence.

Tip

MAKE FRIENDS
Establish a **good rapport** with the audience as early in your talk as possible. **Greet them warmly;** ask them how they are **enjoying** the day. Let them know that you fully understand their issues and that you have the answers.

In focus

ESTABLISHING YOUR CREDIBILITY
Credibility is everything. Your audience needs to buy into you in order to buy into your message. Introducing yourself (or being introduced) with your academic or professional credentials in specific fields may help, especially at formal or academic conferences, but credibility isn't just a function of title—it is a product of confidence, preparation, and experience. Explain to your audience what experience you bring to the issue and why you are qualified to speak; then show that you understand the information and can apply it independently. In order to keep your credibility throughout, you will need to show that you want to communicate, and are prepared to work to do so. You don't have to be word-perfect, but you do need to be focused and organized with what you do know. Your preparation and readiness will speak volumes.

The **opening** to your presentation **grabs the attention** of your **audience** and **sets the stage** for **what is to come**

18 minutes is the **optimum length** for a **talk**

Capturing attention

Be yourself at your most engaging. Rehearse your opening many times—out loud and in front of a mirror—and don't be tempted to improvise. Pump it up, but don't force jokes or stories into the opening if it's not in your character. Above all, be audience-centered; find common ground with the audience early on. Try using the tactics listed on the right:

56%

of **people** in one survey **admitted** they were **afraid** of **public speaking**

Elevating endings

You will probably feel relieved as the end of your presentation approaches, but don't be in a rush to finish: your final words are likely to be those that persist longest in your audience's memory. End with a summary of your key points, or deliver a call to action resting on those points, which will make sure they are remembered—in other words, make sure your ending addresses the objectives you had when starting out.

However you choose to end your presentation, make it meaningful and memorable. Don't finish your presentation by introducing new ideas that you don't have time to support.

Tip

BACK IT UP
Always provide **follow-up materials** so that you continue your **dialogue** with the **audience.** Keep these printed materials **concise** and **relevant** to the presentation—too wide a reach can be off-putting.

O Interesting or entertaining **quotes**

O Unusual or startling **statistics**

O Interesting **survey results**

O Short **anecdotes**

O **Personal stories** of experiences or lessons learned

O Outlines of problems and how you would **solve** them

Your **final words** are likely to be those that persist longest in your audience's memory. End with a **summary of your key points**, or deliver **a call to action** resting on those points

CLOSING A PRESENTATION

Do's

Don'ts

O **Ending on a positive note, even if you've delivered negative information**

O **Restating, rather than reexamining, key points in your material**

O **Being concise**

O Ending abruptly without a summary or call to action, or by calling for questions prematurely

O Introducing new information toward the end of your presentation

O Running out of steam or rushing for the finish line

Winning with words

When you make a presentation, your job is to make the audience understand, recall, and respond to your message. Your success as a speaker depends on your delivery of the message, and this cannot be separated from your choice of words, forms of expression, and the mental images that you conjure up as you bring your words to life.

Convincing and persuading

Persuasive speech, or rhetoric, asks that an audience goes beyond passive listening. Its purpose is to elicit agreement—for example, that a crisis is looming and action is necessary—"to avoid crisis, we must...." The tools of rhetoric were developed in classical times by great thinkers such as Plato and Aristotle, for whom verbal artistry was not just a means to an end, but also a way to arrive at truths about politics and justice. Aristotle, for example, relied most heavily on logic to support his arguments, but also recognized the importance of ethos and pathos.

0.3%

of **pitches** to venture capitalists in **Silicon Valley** **succeed** in getting **investment**

Tip

MIX YOUR MESSAGE
A rounded presentation **combines** several different types of arguments—try mixing **ethos and pathos** in your summing up for a **powerful closing.**

LOGIC

EMOTIONS

COMPASSION

APPEAL

REPUTATION

INTEGRITY

REASONING

EVIDENCE

Classical rhetoric		
TYPE OF RHETORIC	CHARACTERISTICS	EXAMPLE
ETHOS	An appeal based on the **integrity and reputation** of the speaker. You may not understand the reasoning, but you **trust** the speaker.	"As a leading orthopedic surgeon, I recommend this child safety seat."
PATHOS	An appeal to the **emotions** of the listener, such as love, compassion, fear, or greed. Often **personalizes** the argument.	"Give your children the protection they deserve with our safety seats."
LOGOS	An appeal to the listener based on **logic.** This would include **evidence and reason.**	"Fatalities drop 37 percent with our safety seats: the conclusion is clear."

"Because" is such a **persuasive word** that people assume a **rational reason** will follow, even if it does not

ALLEGORY:
"I have a dream"

ACRONYMS:
"Audience, Intent, Message—AIM"

USING A MOTIF:
returning to a symbol or visual image throughout your presentation to add continuity.

GROUPING WORDS IN THREES:
"friends, Romans, countrymen"

USING ACTIVE PHRASING

Do's	Don'ts
O "Sales are rising. That's better than we expected"	O "Surpassing our expectations, sales are rising"
O "We're making real progress"	O "Progress is being made"
O "Training is necessary and it fits our timeline"	O "Training, with respect to our current timeline, has been found necessary"
O "We can understand complex ideas if they are presented well"	O "Complex ideas, provided they're presented well, can be understood"

REPETITION:
"Location, location, location"

MNEMONIC:
"Thirty days has September..."

Creating moments
Beyond the use of clear structure and good narratives, there are many verbal techniques to help your audience remember what you say. Use these sparingly to emphasize key points—sprinkling these devices too liberally throughout your presentation will dilute and therefore spoil their effect.

RHETORICAL QUESTIONS:
"Can one product really deliver all these benefits?"

ALLITERATION:
"the sweet smell of success"

PERSONIFICATION:
"This product will be your faithful companion"

Verbal techniques help your audience remember **what you say**

Eliminating interlopers

Many speakers insert a word or syllable to fill what they perceive as an awkward gap. These filler words—er, um, ah, and so on—bubble up because we are all used to two-way conversation. When you pause, the other person speaks, and so on. When you are presenting, there is no feedback and the silence can be unnerving. Practice and awareness of your own habits will help you become comfortable with natural pauses while you consider the right phrasing, but knowing your material is the best defense against needing to use unnecessary words to fill a space.

Certain phrases detract from your authority as a speaker. There is a temptation to inject words like "possibly" and "perhaps" to soften what you are saying, so that you seem less severe. Don't bother. Eliminating such words and phrases will instantly power up your presentation.

"Might be"

"In my opinion"

"Kind of"

"You know?"

"Hopefully"

"So..."

"OK?"

"A little bit"

Tip

HOLD BACK THE PAPERWORK
If you choose to **distribute** printed **handouts** to your audience, do so only after you have completed your oral presentation. This will prevent the audience from becoming distracted.

Case study

THE PERSONAL TOUCH

Steve Jobs, the cofounder of Apple Inc., was widely renowned for his memorable presentation skills. Jobs often fueled his public appearances and speeches with anecdotes that allowed those who are outside his industry to understand and be inspired.

"Because I had dropped out and didn't have to take the normal classes, I decided to take a calligraphy class...None of this had even a hope of any practical application in my life, but ten years later, when we were designing the first Macintosh computer, it all came back to me... It was the first computer with beautiful typography. If I had never dropped in on that single course in college, the Mac would have never had multiple typefaces or proportionally spaced fonts. And... it's likely that no personal computer would have."

Steve Jobs, Commencement Address, Stanford, California, 2005

"Let me tell you a story"

Using narrative

Six of the most powerful words in the English language are "Let me tell you a story." Narratives bring facts and figures into context and lift presentations out of the realm of dry tutorials. They provide a showcase for the presenter to demonstrate real passion and grasp of the issues, particularly if the narrative resonates on a personal level. Crucially, they—like no other device—will captivate the listener.

Learn to use stories effectively, by reading and listening to accomplished storytellers. Draw on your own personal experiences and practice honing them into stories by telling them in informal situations a few times.

Being memorable

Stories can take diverse forms, but to be useful in a presentation they should have two basic elements—the "what happened," or sequence of events, followed by the "lesson learned" or moral, based on those events.

To increase the likelihood further that your audience will retain your message, distribute a printed handout to supplement your oral presentation. It may be a simple reprise of your presentation; it may contain additional information, elaborating on points you have made; or it may be a list of additional reading. A handout is a useful tool (essential in academic environments), as long as it is thoughtfully structured—it should not just be a place to dump your additional research. Always explain the purpose of your handout to your audience, and never assume that it will be read—it is no substitute for your oral presentation.

Introducing visual aids

It is said that a picture is worth a thousand words, and using visual aids in your presentation undoubtedly heightens impact and improves audience retention. In business, the term "visual aid" often reads as shorthand for PowerPoint™ or other presentation software, but you don't need special technology to add visual flair. A simple prop can make an unforgettable point, and flip charts are foolproof, not to mention cheap, and portable.

Preparing to impress

Visuals are of little value unless they clarify and illustrate your message. When planning your presentation, first establish its basic outline; then refer closely to the content to identify the points that would benefit from visual treatment. Consider what kind of visuals will help you communicate your information and where you can use them in your presentation to greatest effect. Will maps help your audience get a handle on locations? Will graphs or pie charts really help them to understand the figures?

Then consider how much time you will need to invest in finding or generating the visual aids—would your effort be better spent refining and practicing your delivery style?

Making an impact with visuals

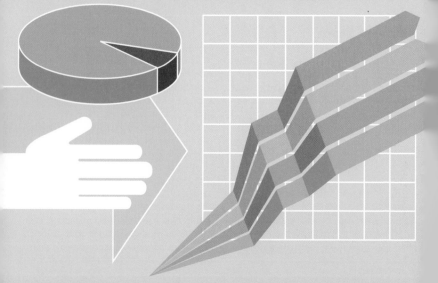

Using props

Some visual aids require little or no preparation. Props are objects that help reinforce a point or grab attention and they are particularly useful if you want to evoke an emotional response. Props can be passed around the audience to engage their senses of smell, touch, and even taste. Use props sparingly, and integrate them well into your presentation so they are not perceived as gimmicks.

Tip

BUILD SUSPENSE
Keep a **prop** covered on the table in front of you before you use it; this will help to create **intrigue** and build **anticipation.**

Consider what **kind of visuals** will help you **communicate your information** and where you can use them in **your presentation** to **greatest effect**

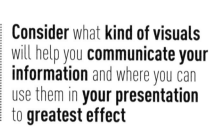

Making images work

The most common presentation tool today is the digital projector, which can be attached to a laptop or other device. Both still images and film need to be used thoughtfully and sparingly; if you bombard your audience with slide after slide, chances are they will retain very little, and a long film presentation is the perfect time to grab a nap.

Remember that the audience needs to be inspired and gain your perspective on the subject. You can only provide these elements yourself.

The **average time** allocated for **a speech is five to seven minutes**

When using an image to make a point, cut down on narration and allow the audience to discover the message for themselves. Don't talk over an image—introduce it. Even a simple photograph of a building will generate more impact than a verbal description alone.

If you bombard your audience with **slide after slide**, chances are they **will retain very little**

The audience needs to be **inspired** and gain **your perspective** on the subject

Using film clips

Think very carefully before using film clips. Most people are used to high production values and as such anything less could work against you. Customer testimonials work very well as film clips, but if you are planning on using a film element you do need to be selective, since the average time allocated for a speech is five to seven minutes. Anything over a couple of minutes of clips and it will appear that your speech is just a distraction for the main event—the film clip!

In focus

RETAINING VISUAL INFORMATION

A study at the University of Pennsylvania's Wharton School of Business found retention rates of verbal-only presentations ran at about **10 percent.** Combining verbal with **visual** messages **increased** retention rates by nearly 400 percent to **50 percent.**

Don't talk over an image—**introduce it**

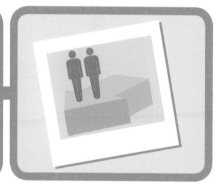

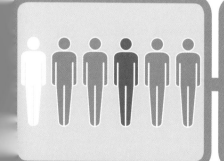

Customer testimonials work very **well** as film clips

Using presentation software

Multimedia projection software has become a standard tool for business presentations. Used with care, the software can greatly enhance the impact of your communication, but beware its seductive nature, which invites you to fill your slides with ever more content and embellishment.

Getting to the point

Creating slides in a dedicated presentation package, such as PowerPoint™ or Keynote™, is easy. But using these tools to communicate effectively is a bigger challenge. First ask yourself if your presentation will actually benefit from slide formatting; it may be just as effective—or more so—to use props, videos, handouts, or just your own voice and authority. For example, slides are not the best way to present lots of data (handouts are much better), but they are effective for showing the relationships between data sets.

Slides are not a magic pill: they won't organize a disorganized presentation; they won't give a point to a presentation that doesn't really have one; and they'll never make a convincing presentation on their own. What your slides can do is reinforce your points, drawing attention to them as you present.

Use no more the **five lines** of **text** per slide

You should let **images** do their own **talking,** and **keep text minimal**

Choosing the cues

When you elect to use multimedia projection tools, use them for what they are good at—showing rather than telling information. Findings from cognitive scientists suggest that because visual and verbal information is processed separately, audiences have a difficult time absorbing both at the same time. This means that you should let images do their own talking, and keep text minimal.

> **Tip**
>
> **KEEP IT SIMPLE**
> If you find yourself apologizing for the **complexity** of a slide, take it out.

Streamlining your content

Less is more. Use your slides to emphasize key points in your presentation rather than as a security blanket—they have far more impact when used sparingly. Don't include complex charts or graphs, assuming people will look at your handouts later to decode them—if a graphic can't be understood during the presentation,

Tip

AVOID "EXTRAS"

If you show it, speak it—don't leave your **audience** wondering why you didn't **address** something on a slide.

Use no more then **six words per line**

take it out or simplify it. Try breaking it into several separate slides; it can be very effective to use a series in which information is "built" with each slide.

Simplify the information on each slide—use no more than five lines of text per slide, and no more than six words per line. Some presenters tend to load their slides with bulleted lists, then deliver their presentation by expanding upon the points. This approach fails to engage the audience; rather than recapping bullet points, try replacing them with intriguing keywords that invite your explanation.

WRITING EFFECTIVE SLIDE TEXT

Do's	Don'ts
O **Using punchy key word bullets, such as: Revolutionary Adaptable**	O Using long bullets or paragraphs of text, such as: Powered by rotary not conventional engine Able to work in temperatures of −15 to 120°F
O **Capitalizing only the first word of each sentence**	O Using all capitals, excessive underlining, or type effects
O **Proofreading your text by reading it backward**	O Using abbreviations or industry jargon

Making great visuals

You don't need to be a graphic designer to produce effective slides. The key—as with text—is to keep things simple, and stick to one, consistent graphic language. Limit yourself to two fonts and two type sizes for the presentation, and use the same conventions throughout—for example, bold text to denote a heading, and italics for quotes. Keep colors and font styles consistent from slide to slide so your audience doesn't have to stop and consider whether any differences are significant to their meaning. Use sans serif fonts—that do not have decorations at the ends of the strokes on letters—for their clarity and clean lines. Consider using white text on dark backgrounds to reduce glare.

Resist the temptation to present every graphic you have access to: use no more than two images on one slide, and no more than three separate curves on one graph. Be imaginative with your images. They don't need to be literal or combined with text—projecting a single, powerful image will help to vary the pace of your presentation and open up discussion.

ASK YOURSELF...
Will my visuals work?   **YES   NO**

1 Will the type you've used be **legible** when projected? **Colors and sizes** may be fine on your computer screen, but not when enlarged by a projector.............................. ☐ ☐

2 Are image **file sizes** manageable? Overly large files tend to load slowly and may stall your presentation........................... ☐ ☐

3 Is the room dark enough for your slides to be seen? Balance the **illumination** in the auditorium so that you can still see your audience, and vice-versa................................. ☐ ☐

4 Is the **type large enough?** A good guide is to add 2 in (5 cm) of character height for every 20 ft (6 m) of distance between your screen and the audience... ☐

Using conventions

Your audience won't have long to interpret complex graphics, so always simplify to the essentials, and take advantage of familiar visual conventions: for example, use the color red to suggest negative numbers, stop, or danger; use pie charts for relative proportions; and use vertical lines to indicate growth. There is no need to reinvent the wheel. Beware of gimmicks, such as animations between slides. Movement is very distracting when processing information, and such effects should be used sparingly.

Keep things **simple,** and stick to one, **consistent** graphic language. Limit yourself to **two fonts** and **two type sizes** for the presentation

How to work with slides

Begin your presentation with a blank slide so that the audience doesn't read ahead.

Walk your audience through each slide following natural **reading patterns** (left to right, top to bottom in Western cultures).

Show slides only when you are **talking** about them. Don't leave them up.

Direct your audience to a slide using a **hand gesture**.

Spend no more than **two minutes** addressing a slide.

When presenting a **complex** slide, allow the audience some time to **absorb the information** before you talk.

Presenting virtually

Fast and near-ubiquitous broadband connections have made the delivery of remote, virtual presentations cheap and reliable—a far cry from the days when video conferencing involved expensive, complex equipment for both the sender and receiver. Getting the best from virtual delivery methods involves combining conventional presenting skills with a new range of techniques.

Benefiting from technology

Delivering your presentation online means your audience can watch, listen, and take part from anywhere in the world. It saves time, travel, and expense, and it appeals increasingly to generations of business people for who the computer has always taken center stage.

> Presentation online means your audience can **watch, listen, and take part** from **anywhere in the world**

Tip

CHECK IT WILL WORK
Always check the **compatibility** of technologies used for remote **conferencing.** Some are dedicated applications that must be installed on the users' computers; some are web-based. The **presenter** may talk over a telephone line, pointing out information being presented on screen, or audio may be incorporated into the software package.

Choosing your format

Web conferencing is the direct descendent of video conferencing, allowing live meetings or presentations to take place over the internet or company intranet. The meeting may be referred to as a webcast, where there is little or no audience participation, or a webinar, where participation is encouraged—via the web, phone, or email. Podcasts can deliver messages that can be viewed on handheld devices or cell phones. All these technologies are increasingly being used to reach staff, investors, and the media, but should always be considered as additions to face-to-face presentation, rather than a replacement. The biggest challenge is keeping your audience engaged when you are not physically present.

7%

of total work time is spent by salespeople **speaking directly** to **clients**

Success in remote presentations

- O Ensure that any **camera angles** show full head shots.

- O Map out your range of movement so that you **stay in frame.**

- O Structure proceedings more **formally** than for an in-person presentation.

- O Begin with a **brief agenda** before making greetings and introductions.

- O Issue regular time checks to **keep on track;** signal breaks well in advance.

- O Don't overanswer questions. **Attention** spans tend to be short.

- O To retain interest, make sure you build in **regular feedback** breaks.

- O Try to **keep things simple** and remind other participants to do so.

- O **Use illustrations,** graphs, and film clips wherever possible.

- O In audio formats, **use repetition** to drive home points.

- O **Acknowledge participants** and give everyone an opportunity to be heard.

Preparing and **practicing**

Every presentation is a performance. The stage needs to be set, the props and costume put in place, lines learned, and delivery rehearsed. Practice is vital to improve confidence and fluency, and to fine-tune your material for oral delivery.

02

Getting word perfect

Don't try to be anyone but yourself. Identify your strengths—humor or storytelling—and put them to good use in your presentation. Practice as much as possible; your audience deserves a presenter who can make the material fresh, understandable, and relevant.

Practicing aloud

Your presentation will be delivered orally, and to reach your confident best, you should practice this way, too. You need literally to deliver your presentation out loud and, if possible, to a test audience that can offer constructive feedback. Run through the presentation in the same (or similar) room or auditorium where you will deliver the real thing, rather than in the car or in your bedroom. Ideally you should run through your presentation out loud five to ten times; this sounds like a lot, but the applause you will receive from your audience will make all the effort worthwhile.

Tip

REHEARSE YOUR ATTITUDE

The **energy** you put into a presentation, and your **enthusiasm** for the subject, will help drive home your message. These apparently **natural characteristics** need practice, too.

Ideally **you should run** through your **presentation** out loud **five to ten** times

In focus

THINKING LIKE A PRESENTER
Growing your presentation skills means thinking like a presenter 24/7. There are many real-life situations where you can develop your skills.

O Practice **narrative techniques** in casual conversations.

O Identify and follow your **natural characteristics** when communicating.

O In **everyday conversation,** watch how your listener responds to different approaches. What works to **keep their attention?**

O Attend presentations by others. Which **styles of presenting** keep your **attention** and which do not?

O Be a collector: **gather anecdotes,** stories, and **quotes** for later use.

O Work on building **one skill at a time.** Before your next presentation, select one area—narrative skills, or presenting statistics, for example. **Concentrate** on improving your delivery in that area.

O Get as much **feedback from your peers** as possible. It is very difficult to evaluate yourself objectively as a communicator.

O **Get targeted feedback.** Ask someone you know to **listen** to your presentation with a specific purpose in mind. Tell them in advance, for example, that you'd like feedback on how strong your eye contact is or how many "filler" words you use.

Honing your delivery

Your goal is to refine your content to make it as powerful as possible and you comfortable enough with your material to set the script aside. Some practice tips are listed below:

With experience, presenters naturally develop their own style of delivery. Some people have a talent for keeping an audience engaged with questions or exercises; others excel at helping an audience understand issues through narrative. No single structure serves all presenters in all circumstances, so it pays to try out many different approaches at different times.

Practice your presentation with an outline, not a full script.

If possible, **practice in front of someone** who has knowledge of the material.

Time your presentation with each round; make sure to stay on track.

After several rehearsals to help you **remember the contents,** practice delivering it without stopping in order to judge its flow.

Absorb your material well enough to give your presentation the look of spontaneity.

After you are satisfied with the content, try **recording a practice round** on video. It will give you a new perspective on how you look and sound to others.

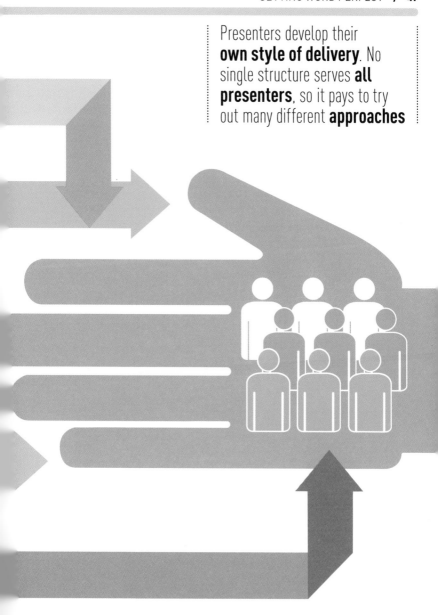

Presenters develop their **own style of delivery**. No single structure serves **all presenters**, so it pays to try out many different **approaches**

Pacing yourself

Effective presenters know that good timekeeping can be as important as good content. A presentation that starts and ends on time gives a strong impression of competence. Achieving this goal is the result of excellent preparation, making time for rehearsal and flexibility on the day.

Preparing notes

A formal presentation or speech is the wrong place for an original thought. Effective communicators plan, prepare, and practice their material. Most presenters use notes. Even if you don't need to consult them, they can be reassuring. Treat them as prompts rather than a script. Write them in the form of bullet points or keywords, not complete sentences, and rehearse "joining up" the points. Don't worry if your words aren't the same every time.

Notes are most useful when they are accessible at any point during the presentation. Use numbered sheets or cards, ensuring that your numbers match up with handouts or slides. Your notes can also serve as a backup if you can't use your visual aids.

If you do need to refer to notes, don't try to hide it. Take a moment, review your material, and continue. Your audience will take the pause in their stride.

2 minutes is the time it takes to read **one page** of **double-spaced** text to an **audience**

Timekeeping tips

- Never, ever go over your **allotted time.** Your audience will thank you.

- Watch your **breathing.** If you are running out of breath, **slow down your delivery.**

- If you tend to **speak** too quickly, try delivering each point to one person, **maintaining eye contact** with them before allowing yourself to move on.

- It takes about **two minutes** to deliver a page of double-spaced text.

- When **rehearsing,** remember that the **pace** of the actual presentation will probably be slower due to summarizing, natural pauses, and nerves. Compensate by erring on the side of less material, rather than more.

Effective communicators **plan, prepare,** and **practice** their material. Most **presenters** use notes

Tip

Recruit a timekeeper
Placing a friendly person as **"timekeeper"** in the audience who can unobtrusively signal the **time** remaining to you is a good way to **stay on track.**

O Don't use automatic scrolling features for projected slides. The **presenter,** not the technology, should **set the pace.**

O Practice using a **stopwatch**—don't rely on guesswork or estimates.

O If a colleague is going to "drive" the slides for you, **practice your timing** together so you don't have to say, "next slide, please."

O Interactivity is an **advanced skill,** because it complicates **pacing.** If you use it, consider imposing a limit on the number of questions, or group them together by saying, "I see there are a lot of questions here. If you would, hold your questions and I will address them after this section."

Being spontaneous

Planning for spontaneity appears, at first, to be a contradiction. But building in opportunities to digress from the main path of your presentation allows you to shine in front of your audience, making you appear the master of your material, and so helping to retain attention.

Making room for digression

Memorizing your presentation word-for-word is not a good idea. Unless you are a skilled actor, your delivery is likely to be flat and uninteresting. The same goes for reading from a script; listeners may misjudge your authorship, or question your commitment to your words. Instead, practice your material so that you know it so well you can deviate from it with confidence. By all means use short notes as prompts, but plan moments into your presentation where you can elaborate on a point of interest, or talk with great passion about an area very close to your heart. Digressions are very useful tools since they can provide "oases"—places where you can take a short respite from the focused intensity of your presentation to talk about topics you know inside-out. These moments will give you a breather and allow you to relax and regain your poise before continuing.

Plan moments into your presentation to **elaborate** on a **point of interest**

Tip

KEEP ON TRACK
Treat any digression as a **chance to connect** with the audience. Move from behind the desk or lectern, and make **eye contact** with the audience as you speak. Your audience will perceive your delivery as one-of-a-kind—a presentation tailored to them.

Using levity

Humor can be a powerful icebreaker, and used carefully, will demonstrate that you are attending to your audience because you are sensitive to what they find amusing. If you choose to use humor, be careful how you do so. The wrong joke or story that may have seemed funny at the time can easily backfire and cause irreparable harm to how you are perceived by your audience. The benefits and drawbacks of humor are magnified tenfold when presenting to culturally different audiences: a timely joke will light up the audience and show that you have made an effort to understand their perspective; conversely, an inappropriate joke can be disastrous.

Remember that using humor is not essential, and if you don't feel natural being funny, don't try. Similarly, if you have any doubts about the suitability of a joke or type of humor, just leave it out rather than risking offense.

83%

of **viewers** in one survey enjoyed commercials that **made them laugh**

PRESENTING WITH HUMOR

Do's

- **Rehearsing your jokes**
- **Turning humor on yourself and being self-deprecating**
- **Employing humor sparingly to lighten a mood or diffuse tension**
- **Using humor that flows naturally from your own experiences**

Don'ts

- Forcing humor if it does not come naturally to you
- Being sarcastic or making jokes that may embarrass others
- Relying on jokes so much that your message becomes diluted
- Using humor that depends on context or detailed explanation

Planning the practicalities

The physical environment has a significant impact on the way you communicate and connect with your audience. The success of your presentation depends crucially on whether people can hear and see it clearly. So make sure you consider the physical space in which you will present and the equipment you will need.

Assessing the location

The practical side of your presentation demands as much foresight as the content itself. Don't leave the details to others, on the assumption that everyone knows what is required to make your presentation a success. Instead, plan ahead and give yourself enough time on the day to ensure everything is well prepared and make final adjustments. If possible, view the venue and layout (see opposite) well in advance, and arrange a meeting with the facility's manager to request any necessary changes.

> **Tip**
>
> **CHECK LINES OF SIGHT**
> If you are using **visual aids,** consider whether everyone will have a **clear view** of them, bearing in mind where you will be standing as you describe them.

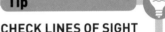

View **the venue** and **layout in advance**

Layout pros and cons

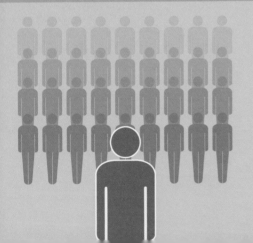

CLASSROOM

The classroom-style layout features rows of seating, perhaps with desks or tables.

PROS: Ideal for larger audiences; desks make it easy to take notes.

CONS: Less conducive to interactivity; people finding or leaving their seats can be disruptive.

CHECKLIST...
Scoping out the venue

YES **NO**

1 Will everyone be able **to see and hear** the presentation from all vantage points in the room? ☐ ☐

2 Can you be **heard at the back** of the room? Take someone with you to help check. ☐ ☐

3 Can you **control the lighting** in the room, if necessary? ☐ ☐

4 Can **windows** be shaded to eliminate glare? ☐ ☐

5 Are **power points** conveniently located? ☐ ☐

6 Is there a **table for handouts,** business cards, or follow-up information? ☐ ☐

7 Will **additional seating** be available if needed? ☐ ☐

8 Will a **sound system** be necessary for audience questions? ☐ ☐

9 Is all audiovisual equipment tested and in good working order, and are you happy that you know how to use it? ☐ ☐

CHEVRON OR WING LAYOUT

This is similar to the classroom style, but the seating is split into blocks angled toward the presenter.

PROS: Audience is brought closer to the presenter; better potential for interactivity.

CONS: Takes more space for fewer seats compared with classroom style.

Using lasers

Any tool or device that helps audience understanding is worth considering. Laser pointers are widely used by presenters to direct a thin beam of light at a screen or other medium. They can be useful for highlighting a particular area of a slide or other visual aid without obscuring the image with your own hand or a physical pointer.

However, bear in mind that if your visual material is too busy or complicated to be understood without you using a pointer to explain it, there may be a case for simplifying it, or perhaps assigning the various points to more than one slide. If you use a laser pointer, make sure you keep it directed away from the audience to avoid a distracting light show.

Layout pros and cons

HORSESHOE

Audience members are arranged in curved rows around the presenter.

PROS: Ideal for smaller groups; good for interaction; good lines of sight; provides work space for audience.

CONS: This layout can only accommodate a limited number of seats.

Using remotes

Wireless remote controls allow presenters to advance to the next slide without having to stand right next to the equipment. Since this gives you the physical freedom to move around, it can help you achieve the right level of interaction with your audience and deliver a professional, free-flowing presentation.

Laser pointers can be useful for **highlighting** a **particular area** of a **slide** or other **visual aid** without obscuring the **image** with a physical pointer

92.6%

of people claim the **visual aspect** is the important factor in **choosing** a product

Tip

CHOOSE SIDES
If you are **right-handed,** stand to the **left** of your screen or flipchart so you don't have to reach across your own body when **pointing.** If you are left-handed, stand to the right.

BOARDROOM

Audience members are seated around a long table, with the presenter at the head.

PROS: Generates a sense of formality.

CONS: Some seats have poor lines of sight, making prolonged viewing and listening uncomfortable; showing visuals can be awkward for the same reason.

Making yourself heard

If you know you will be speaking with a microphone and public-address system, make sure you arrive early to allow time for a sound check. Your goal is to make sure you will be heard clearly around the room, over the level of normal background noise.

Practice projecting your voice to fill the room's farthest corners without shouting, and without getting too close to the microphone.

Remember, microphones only amplify your voice; they don't improve your delivery. The rhythm, pitch, and expression of your voice need to be as carefully controlled as in any other situation.

25%

decrease in **voice pitch** is thought to increase the **success** of CEOs and politicians

Microphones **only amplify** your voice; they don't improve your delivery. **The rhythm, pitch, and expression** of your voice need to be **carefully** controlled

Tip

ASK FOR QUIET
Before you start, ask for all phones and electronic devices to be turned off, and make sure noise from nearby rooms or hallways is abated.

Microphone technique

O Don't **tap** the microphone to test it—**speak** into it

O Don't get so **close** that you "pop your P's" or amplify your breath

O Keep **jewelry, hair,** and **buttons** away from the microphone

O Don't pound or tap the **lectern** or rustle papers near the microphone

O Keep your voice **natural** and **varied**

O Do check with your audience, even after the initial **sound check,** to make sure everyone can hear

Selecting a microphone

Choose the type of microphone suited to the mode of your presentation. Handheld models allow presenters to move while speaking, but limit gestures to your free hand. Lavaliere microphones solve that problem: they can be secured to clothes, and wireless models allow for even greater freedom of movement. However, they must be placed correctly to avoid volume drop-off as you turn your head. Stationary microphones work well if you are using a podium, but limit movement. Whatever your choice, make sure you practice positioning and projection beforehand. On the day, ensure you know when your microphone is on, and how to turn it off.

Respecting other cultures

All cultures have their own unique customs and rules, particularly when it comes to speaking and interacting in formal and work settings. While those from outside the culture are generally given some latitude, it is wise to consider any relevant cultural issues before you present.

Knowing the norms

Presenting in a foreign country can be a daunting experience. On top of all the usual issues of preparation, you must deliver your material in an unfamiliar place and setting. However, you can still build rapport with your audience by doing some prior research into basic rules of conduct, or "norms," and how they differ from those of your native culture.

> **Build rapport** with your **audience** by doing some prior research into basic **rules of conduct** and how they differ from those of your **native culture**

Understanding cultures

Emphasizing points through a strong voice and definitive hand gestures is a sign of confidence in the United States. In the UK, however, this style may come across as abrasive—and in China, it could seem vulgar. Passing a microphone over someone's head or pointing to a member of the audience may be perfectly acceptable in most Western cultures, but it's the height of rudeness in Thailand.

Tip

GET UP TO SPEED QUICKLY
If you can, get some basic **cultural information** from your **hosts,** then supplement this knowledge with additional resources such as guidebooks and websites.

ASK YOURSELF...
Am I appropriate?   **YES NO**

1 Am I using the **proper forms** of address?.................................. ☐ ☐

2 Have I adhered to the **appropriate standards** of dress?................. ☐ ☐

3 Am I aware of any idioms or slang I use?
Can I avoid using them while presenting? .... ☐ ☐

4 Do I know which hand gestures or **body language**
are appropriate and inappropriate to use? .... ☐ ☐

5 Are my visuals **clear** and simple enough to **express**
my message even if my audience doesn't understand
everything I say 100 percent?.. ☐ ☐

6 Have I run my presentation past a person **familiar** with
local culture before the big day? .... ☐ ☐

While **direct eye contact** is valued as **a sign** of trustworthiness in many **Western** societies, it is generally considered rude in **India** and **South Asia**

Learning how to act

While direct eye contact is generally valued as a sign of trustworthiness in many Western societies, it is generally considered rude in India and South Asia. Western-style "casual Fridays," when dress codes are relaxed, may be regarded as unprofessional in other parts of the world. Bare legs for women may be considered normal and practical in some cultures, but unprofessional or offensive in others.

In the United States, Canada, and Australia, the use of first names in business settings is very common. However, in Hong Kong, Portugal, and Germany, using first names without being invited to do so is considered overly familiar.

Solving problems

Planning for problems isn't negative thinking. It is simply common sense. Consider the industries that devote enormous resources to preparing for unfortunate events that they hope will never occur. From airlines to utilities, it is a wise policy to expect the unexpected and arm yourself to handle problems with ease.

Preparing a "Plan B"

Even the most carefully crafted presentations will come up against unexpected technical or human problems. Glitches in equipment, logistical delays, or lack of preparation on the part of others may conspire to upset your plans. It pays to plan for problems, and develop a "Plan B" for every eventuality.

When a problem occurs, you need to act fast. Don't waste time apologizing or fretting out loud about the disruption,

Displaying a **calm** disposition in front of your **audience** will **pay dividends**

When you rehearse your presentation, identify topics that you can leave out if you have been allocated less time than you had expected; similarly, plan an audience discussion or question and answer session that you can quickly and easily deploy if you run short. Your audience will tend to take their cues from you. If you take any mishap or change of plans in your stride, so will they. Displaying a cool head and calm disposition in front of your audience will pay off in the end. If there is a mishap, show that you are fully in control and you will get right back on track through body language and your words and actions.

How to stop a phone pest

just continue as if nothing has happened, by putting your "Plan B" into action. Always make sure you are one step ahead and have thought of everything. If your computer presentation fails, for example, fall back on the note cards you prepared containing your key messages. Better still, carry an extra laptop as well as a spare projector bulb.

Request that **all phones** are switched off before you start.

Handling interruption

There is usually no need to stop your presentation for latecomers—continue speaking while they take their seats. However, there are exceptions. If a key decision-maker arrives late, pause and provide a quick summary to bring that person up to speed. Make sure it is brief enough so the latecomer does not feel embarrassed. Be ready to handle interruptions of all kinds: the most common of these is the ringing cell phone. If you notice audience members using phones or other electronic devices, others will almost certainly notice too; such distractions can quickly disrupt and undermine your presentation.

If it happens again, **call a break** and speak privately to the offender.

If the **owner picks up the call,** pause and wait quietly until he/she has dealt with it.

If **a phone then rings,** don't try to speak over it. Pause, let the owner switch it off, and **stay calm.**

Stop the talk

If you can hear chatter or side conversations, pause. This will draw attention to the culprits who will hopefully realize they are at fault and stop. If they persist, don't single out individuals, but ask firmly if there are any questions that the audience wishes to raise. Add that everyone will want to devote their full attention to the next part of the presentation because it contains some very important information.

Recovering poise

There are times when you will find yourself—briefly—lost for words. It can happen to anyone; even actors forget their lines from time to time. Don't panic—you know your material, so skip ahead or summarize what you have covered already: it will appear to the audience to be part of a well-planned delivery. There are tried and tested techniques that will buy you a few moments to get back on track. Try one of the following for a quick recovery. Stay calm, and you won't lose momentum:

- Repeat the last thing you said
- Return to a key message
- Pause and review your notes
- Ask the audience if they have any questions
- Use your visuals as a prompt
- Call for a break.

Being ready for the moment

The number one strategy for boosting presentation skill is to devote as much time as you can to preparation and practice. Don't take shortcuts. By doing the work in advance, you can make your presentation work for you and communicate successfully every time.

Making final checks

Run through your presentation perhaps once or twice, either alone or with a "friendly" audience. You are looking to reaffirm your material, not pick holes in it. You may feel the temptation to rework everything from top to bottom. Resist this urge and stick with the ideas you have developed over time—there is no time to assess the implications of any big changes. Check your visual aids one last time, making sure you are up to speed with all the practicalities of your presentation. Again, don't be tempted to make any major changes at the last minute.

Am I confident that I am making my "best case"?

Do I believe everything I am saying?

Could I deliver this presentation without any materials or notes if I had to?

Have I anticipated any questions I might get?

Tip

PRACTICE THE TRANSITIONS
If **rehearsal time** is short, spend it **practicing** your transitions from one point to another, rather than delivering details. Getting these moments **right** will make your presentation appear **much smoother.**

Is there any part of my presentation I couldn't fully explain if I had more time?

Am I ready?

Have I vetted the information I am presenting with others?

Do I fully understand my audience's expectations?

?

Am I ready with follow-up or additional information?

Do I know what next steps are called for?

Am I looking forward to this presentation or dreading it?

Speaking at short notice

There may be times when you have to prepare or alter a presentation at very short notice. In this situation, the overriding concern is to use whatever time you do have to best effect.

Focus on your key messages rather than supporting details, and write them into a streamlined one-page outline.

Prepare for likely questions, but forget about creating elaborate visuals—you will more often than not get bogged down in layout rather than content. Use existing materials, or do without. When you give the presentation, explain the situation to the audience and offer to answer their questions as best you can, and provide additional material should it be needed.

Taking
center stage

As your presentation approaches, all the preparation you have put into your material and delivery may be overshadowed by the prospect of having to perform. Don't worry. There are plenty of techniques that will give you a real advantage on the day of your presentation, boost your confidence, and help you deal with nerves or mishaps.

Creating a first impression

The first thing your audience will notice is how you look, and this first impression is hard to change. Give plenty of thought to the message you want to send through your attire, grooming, and posture. Study yourself in a mirror, and ask colleagues for their opinion on your appearance.

Connecting with the audience

Appearance alone won't win over your audience, but it plays an important role in setting out your intent and credibility. When choosing what to wear, consider which outfit will have the greatest influence on the people you would like to impress the most.

For example, if the audience consists mostly of your casually dressed peers, but also includes two suited directors, dress up not down. And if you are the manager of a factory addressing the factory floor, think how differently your message will be perceived if you are wearing a suit or clean corporate coveralls.

Tip

LOOK SHARP
Change into a **fresh, pressed** outfit just before you begin your presentation; **check** beforehand that changing facilities are available.

ASK YOURSELF...

	YES	NO
1 Is my **hair clean,** neatly styled, and away from my face?	☐	☐
2 Are my **fingernails** clean and trimmed?	☐	☐
3 Have I **trimmed** my beard and moustache?	☐	☐
4 Are any potentially offensive tattoos visible?	☐	☐
5 Is my **perfume/cologne** overpowering? Many people find scent unappealing, so it should be avoided	☐	☐
6 Have I **applied** antiperspirant?	☐	☐

Dressing to impress

There are no fixed rules about dress and appearance, but if unsure, veer toward neat, professional, and conservative rather than trying to reassure your audience by "blending in" with their style. You are dressing to create an air of authority and confidence rather than to please yourself, so steer clear of casual clothes like jeans and sneakers, leather, shiny fabrics, and anything with prominent emblems or designer labels. Avoid distracting blocks of bright color, though color can be used to provide an accent. Make sure your shoes are clean, polished, but comfortable—if it is painful to stand in them for the length of the presentation, change them.

Minimize jewelry—you don't want your accessories to be the most memorable part of your presentation—and always pay attention to details, even if you won't get that close to the audience. You can bet that they'll notice if your clothes are wrinkled or your cuffs are frayed. Remove bulging keys, change, and other loose items from all your pockets, and check that your lapels are free from any name tags.

Whatever your dress, always take the time to groom yourself—your audience will not forgive an unkempt appearance or poor personal hygiene.

Tip

KEEP IT REAL
It is important to feel at ease while presenting. While you shouldn't forsake **style** for comfort, avoid wearing clothes so **formal** that they make you feel self-conscious and false.

Looking confident

The audience is on your side—they want you to succeed; they want to learn and be inspired by you. But to win their attention and trust, and to exert your influence, you need to impose your presence and demonstrate confidence in yourself and in your presentation material.

Growing self-belief

Inner confidence comes from a combination of self-belief and real enthusiasm for your message. When you are confident, you behave naturally, and in the full expectation of a positive outcome; your self-assurance is genuine and the audience buys into your message.

You can build your confidence over time through exercises in which you visualize success and, of course, through experience. Looking confident and feeling confident may seem two very different things to you, but to your audience, they are one and the same. Employing techniques that make you appear more confident will bring positive feedback from your audience, which will boost inner confidence.

Tip

ACCENTUATE THE POSITIVE
Refrain from **crossing** your arms or leaning backward, away from the **audience;** these **actions** send out very strong negative signals.

When you are **confident,** you **behave naturally,** and in the **full expectation** of a **positive outcome**

Establishing your presence

You can win the attention and respect of an audience before you begin simply through your posture, and by the way you occupy the space around you. Even if you cannot rearrange the seating in the room, you should become familiar with the room, your position, and the lines of sight—"owning" the space will make you feel more comfortable and confident. Give yourself room to move, and make sure the audience can see your hands; don't trap yourself behind a desk or use the lectern as a shield—the audience may interpret your position as defensive.

Tip

USE PROPS
If nerves deter you from using your body, **hold a prop**—such as a pen or wireless remote—in one hand until you find your comfort level and **confidence.**

1/10
of a **second** is all it takes for people to **assess** each other

ASK YOURSELF...
Do I appear confident?   **YES   NO**

1 Is my **eye contact** strong? .... ☐ ☐

2 Am I projecting my **voice?** .... ☐ ☐

3 Am I maintaining **good posture?** .... ☐ ☐

4 Are my **hand gestures** natural? .... ☐ ☐

5 Is my **language** conversational? .... ☐ ☐

6 Are my **movements** purposeful? .... ☐ ☐

7 Do I appear **calm** and in control? .... ☐ ☐

Using body language

If your content is irrelevant or your delivery dull, you shouldn't be surprised if your audience switches off. But they will also disengage if the nonverbal messages that you send out are

inconsistent with your words. Your stance, gestures, and eye contact must support what you say; in the event of any conflicting information, the audience will tend to believe what your body language appears to be saying.

Start your presentation with a neutral but authoritative posture. Maintain a balanced stance, with your feet slightly apart and your weight spread evenly between them. Keep upright, facing the front, with shoulders straight, not hunched, and your arms loosely and comfortably at your sides. Don't lean on a chair or perch on furniture for support.

Timing your movement
For the first 30 seconds of your presentation, try not to move your feet. This "anchoring" will help establish your authority with your audience. As you build rapport, you can relax your posture—this will help win you trust and make the audience feel much more comfortable—leaning forward sends a positive and friendly message.

In focus

THE 7-38-55 RULE
According to a study by Dr. Albert Mehrabian of the University of California, how much we like someone when we first meet them depends only 7 percent on what they say. Tone of voice accounts for 38 percent. The remaining 55 percent is body language and facial expression. This is known as the 7-38-55 rule.

> Your **stance, gestures, and eye contact** must support what you say, **the audience** will believe your **body language**

30
seconds at the **start** of your presentation should be spent standing in a **balanced stance**

Tip

SPRING-CLEAN YOUR BAD HABITS
Rid your **performance** of any visible signs of discomfort you may be **feeling.** Avoid nervous mannerisms such as putting your hands stiffly behind your back, looking down at the floor, playing with jewelry or hair or fiddling with your sleeves or buttons.

Moving for effect

Human attention is drawn to movement—it is programmed into our genes—so one of the most powerful ways to hold on to your audience, and to make viewers focus on you, is to move.

Always use movement purposefully and intentionally—if you merely walk back and forth it will be interpreted as nervous pacing and will distract the audience. However, using movement in tandem with words will boost impact. Listed below are a few examples where actions will reinforce the message:

When you want to refer the audience to **a projected slide,** step back toward it, and sweep your arm to **guide the viewer's eyes** up toward the slide: be careful not to turn your back on your audience as you move.

Move to a different spot on the stage area when **moving from point to point**—this can help the audience to separate out your **key messages.**

Coordinate your movements to **emphasize an important point**—for example, walk across the room, and turn quickly to coincide with the conclusion of a point.

Your movements need not be too theatrical—your goal is to **hold the attention of the audience** rather than to entertain them.

> You may need to **"amplify" small movements** to take into **account the scale** of a room

Using gestures

Use gestures to reinforce points, just as you would in casual conversation; you may need to "amplify" small movements to take into account the scale of a room: for example, a hand gesture may need to become a movement of the whole forearm if it is to be seen from the back. You may need to practice to make such gestures appear "natural." Avoid at all costs any intimidating gestures, such as pointing fingers at your audience or forcefully banging your hand or fist on the table or lectern.

Making eye contact

Many presenters deliberately avoid making eye contact with the audience. But if you can keep your nerve, engaging with the audience in this way creates trust and intimacy, and is one of the most effective means of keeping attention, especially throughout a longer presentation.

95%

of an audience thought the **style** of a talk was equally **important** as the **content**

SHAKING HANDS CONFIDENTLY

Do's	Don'ts
O **Bending your elbow and extending your right arm**	O Offering just the fingers of your hand
O **Pumping your hand two or three times before releasing**	O Holding on to the other person's hand too long or too lightly
O **Making and keeping eye contact with the person you are greeting**	O Looking around the room while shaking someone's hand

Keeping a connection

Unless you are presenting to a very large group, attempt to make eye contact with every member of the audience at least once. Maintain contact for no more than three seconds—longer contact may be seen as hostile. If you find this unnerving, start by making eye contact with someone who looks friendly and approachable before moving around the rest of the room.

Remember also to target people at the back and sides, or those who appear less enthusiastic. If you remain too nervous, look between two heads or scan the room—never avert your eyes from the audience. Not only will you lose their trust, but your voice may become muffled and indistinct, too.

Holding the audience

Novelty and expectation will keep your audience focused through the early parts of your presentation. But keeping their attention once they are accustomed to the sound of your voice and your presentation style can be more of a challenge. Look for signs of disengagement, and be prepared to act quickly to bring the audience back on track.

Keeping interest

You have prepared an interesting presentation. You are delivering it with conviction using a good range of visual materials and rhetorical devices. Yet when you look out, you don't get the reassurance of attentive expressions on the faces of the audience; you may even detect signs of distraction.

Perhaps your audience is tired, or your presentation is the last in a grueling day, or maybe you are delivering some difficult material. In any case, you need to take action fast:

- **Ask the audience** if they can hear and understand your words and if they are comfortable. Take remedial steps if necessary.

Reading signs from the audience

POSITIVE SIGNS

- Chin resting on hand
- Legs relaxed and parallel
- Clasped fingers
- Making eye contact
- Nodding in agreement
- Leaning forward

Tip

MONITOR THE MAJORITY

Regularly **assess** your **audience** for signs of discontent or agitation, but remember that isolated displays of **body language** may be misleading, and they can vary between **cultures.**

Get **interactive and pose questions** to the audience and **invite answers**

- **Consciously change** your delivery; slow your pace, or introduce pauses after key points. Change your pitch or volume.
- **Get interactive** and pose questions to the audience and invite answers. Field questions. Leave your position behind the podium and walk out into the audience, making extensive eye contact.
- **Don't get frustrated** with the audience. Compliment them so that they feel valued.
- **Tell your audience** what's coming up, and when—"we'll work through a few examples before moving on to a question and answer session in five minutes." This will help them feel more involved in proceedings.

NEGATIVE SIGNS

- O Tapping feet
- O Crossing legs
- O Talking to a neighbor
- O Looking around the room
- O Folding arms across the chest
- O Leaning away from the speaker

Calming nerves

Public speaking ranks at the top of many people's list of worst fears. Be assured that this fear is understandable and normal—and even highly experienced presenters sometimes feel some anxiety. Rather than fighting your fear, try to harness it so it works for you; as ever, this requires preparation, practice, and persistence.

Channeling your energy

Before your presentation, you will be brimming with nervous energy. Start by giving that energy a release: vent any concerns to a trusted colleague, then go for a walk, or do some gentle stretching and warm-up exercises. Your body's physical response to stress tends to work against your mental preparations.

In focus

RITUALS AND CONFIDENCE

Repeating the same sequence of actions and thoughts before each presentation is a helpful tool in preventing nerves. Rituals are used by people to combat much stronger fears—such as agoraphobia and fear of flying—because they set up a safe zone of familiarity. Your ritual can be anything from cleaning your glasses to arranging your papers geometrically on the desk—just make sure that it is a sequence of simple, undemanding tasks that won't cause stress themselves.

Tip

CONTROL THE SYMPTOMS

There are many **symptoms** of nerves: feeling "butterflies" in your stomach is common, as is dryness of the mouth; twitching eyes; fidgeting or playing with your hair or a pen; and rocking from side to side. Work on **controlling** the **external signs** so they are not visible to your audience.

Take the following preventative action before you begin your presentation:

- Take several deep breaths, holding each for a count of four, then slowly release through your mouth. This will help moderate a quickening pulse and heartbeat.
- Don't take your position too early. Keep your body moving in the moments just before your presentation.
- Shrug your shoulders to help ease tension.
- Give your voice a warm-up by humming; stretch and release your facial muscles.

Letting yourself shine

Once you begin the presentation, control the release of energy. Don't dissipate it too early by pacing around or rushing your delivery. Maintain eye contact with individuals in the audience; this will help your nerves because it gives you a mental focus, and you will probably get positive feedback from your audience (smiles and nodding heads) that will boost your confidence. Behavioral research has found visualizing a stressful event is enough to trigger a real physical reaction. Conversely, we can all achieve a calmer state through positive images. So, before your next presentation, try visualizing your own success.

Public speaking is ranked the **3rd most frightening experience** in the **US;** in the **UK,** it ranked 2nd

How to visualize success

Tell yourself you are well prepared. **You CAN do it!**

Imagine yourself taking the stage **confidently** and **speaking well.** See yourself **enjoying** the moment.

Remember how you feel at your most **confident.** Tell yourself you can and will **succeed.**

Tell yourself you don't need to be **perfect;** the audience is on **your side.**

Picture yourself as **relaxed and prepared**— you look more confident than you feel.

Speaking powerfully

How do you sound? In control? Authoritative? Dynamic? Voice is a powerful tool in the presentation arsenal. Don't worry—you don't need to have the booming resonance of a stage actor to convince your audience that you are fully involved in what you are saying.

Using confident vocals

As you speak, your audience "reads" your voice—its nuances of pitch, volume, pace, and so on. This process happens imperceptibly, below the radar of consciousness, yet it shapes your audience's perceptions of your message. Sound hesitant and your audience will question your content. Sound confident and your audience will side with you. Try using the various facets of your voice (see right) when you practice your presentation and use them to effect.

INTONATION
Using an upward inflection (upspeak) at the end of sentences may signal you are uncertain. Using **declarative sentences** with the voice ending in a downbeat will give even neutral phrases an **authoritative** touch.

PACE
Vary the pace of your delivery. This helps keep your audience alert. Speak slowly when delivering **key** messages: **new ideas** need time to be processed.

Remaining calm

Slow and deep breathing enhances your performance. It boosts the supply of oxygen to your brain, making you more alert; it helps you stay calm; and it increases the flow of air over your vocal cords, enhancing the clarity of your voice. To keep from stumbling during your presentation, declutter your speech by removing unnecessary words and any trite expressions.

Finally, learn to be comfortable with silence in front of an audience: it feels odd at first, but remember that "dramatic pauses" after key points add memorable emphasis.

TONE
Whether **presenting** good or bad information, do so with a **tone** that matches the content of what you are saying.

Master your voice

VOLUME

Be comfortable **projecting your voice** so that it can be heard everywhere in the room. Vary your projection to grab and **keep attention.** Your goal is not only to be heard, but also to **alert** listeners to the importance of what you are saying.

DICTION

Enunciate words clearly, adjusting the pace of your **delivery** where needed. Be careful with acronyms or unusual words your audience might misunderstand. Repeat important numbers for emphasis and to be certain they are heard.

PITCH

Slow your delivery and breathe deeply. Only then will you be able to use the **full range** of highs and lows of your voice. A confident speaker **varies pitch** more than a rushed one, whose pitch is flat and unengaging.

Tip

PROTECT YOUR VOICE
Don't drink milk or milk products before speaking—they will coat your mouth. **Rest your voicebox** (larynx) for at least a day before your presentation, and take **regular** sips of **water** while speaking.

Sound confident and your audience will **side with you**

Succeeding with formal speeches

Formal speeches such as keynote addresses, appearances at award ceremonies, and addresses to trade conferences and plenary sessions follow structured formats and are often delivered in large group settings. Look on them less as a chance to inform—more to entertain your audience while enhancing your own reputation.

Crafting your content

Delivering a formal speech at an official or ceremonial occasion requires a particular method of preparation. Formal speeches may be read verbatim from a script, delivered from detailed cards, or delivered extemporaneously based on careful preparation. However, they lack important features of other presentations: visual aids are rarely used, and the speaker is physically separated from the audience, limiting the degree of interaction.

As with other presentations, consider who will be in the audience and what they need, as well as the messages you want the audience to receive.

Tip

KEEP DOWN THE DETAIL

There is a limit to the **level of detail** people can **absorb** while listening as opposed to reading. **Test your speech** on someone who hasn't heard it and check that they understand.

59%

of presentations in one survey were **appreciated** for their **clarity,** followed by **pace**

Speaking naturally

Match your delivery to the nature of the occasion; evening receptions, for example, are not the time for complex content—the audience is more inclined to be entertained. Without visual aids, handouts, or interactivity, your words must carry the full weight of your message. Keep your sentences short and confine yourself to one point per sentence.

Emulate the natural rhythms of speech in your script, keeping your sentences flowing naturally. Although the occasion may be formal, don't use "sophisticated" vocabulary solely to try to impress your audience. Instead, use everyday language in a concise and accurate way.

Adapting your delivery style

Even though you will probably be reading your speech, look for different ways in which you can show personality and commitment to your message. Use hand gestures as you would naturally when you speak, to emphasize your points. A simple device such as this will help to keep things interesting for your audience.

Don't feel you have to read each word or phrase exactly as written. You should feel free to depart from your speech as required; this will give your delivery a much more spontaneous feel. Aim for a style of delivery that does not call attention to itself, but that conveys your ideas clearly and precisely without distracting the audience.

Tips for speaking with confidence

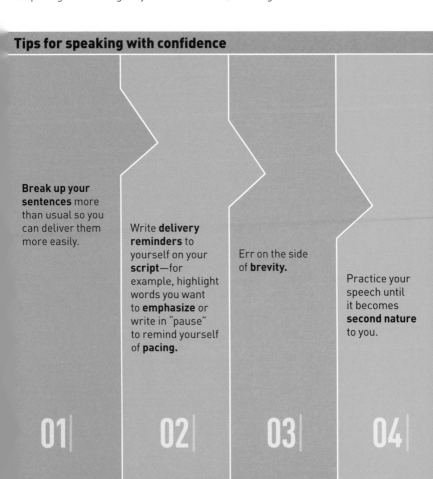

Break up your sentences more than usual so you can deliver them more easily.

01

Write **delivery reminders** to yourself on your **script**—for example, highlight words you want to **emphasize** or write in "pause" to remind yourself of **pacing.**

02

Err on the side of **brevity.**

03

Practice your speech until it becomes **second nature** to you.

04

38%

of the degree we **like** people is due to their **tone of voice**

> **Tip**
>
> **ACT NATURAL**
> To make your **delivery** more human and **natural**, imagine a member of the audience (or a friend) on the other side of the teleprompter.

Tips for speaking with confidence

Practice reading ahead so you can speak with your **eyes on the audience** for as long as possible.

05

If someone else has drafted your speech, rewrite or **adapt** it so that it **reflects your own "voice."** Add a few personal references to make it seem **less formal.**

06

Visualize yourself as a **professional TV host**—try to inhabit the role.

07

Ask for and **learn** from **feedback.**

08

Using teleprompters

Text-display devices such as hidden screens and teleprompters can avoid the need for a podium. They allow you to appear more fully engaged with your audience by looking in their general direction as you read and delivering your text more naturally.

However, it takes practice to use these devices well. You need to be sufficiently at ease with them, so they aren't a distraction, either to you or your audience.

Teleprompters allow you to appear **more fully engaged** with your audience by **looking** in their general direction and **delivering your text more naturally**

How to use teleprompters

Follow these simple steps in order to ensure a smooth, professional performance:

O Teleprompters do vary. **Rehearse** with the actual device you will be using.

O As with every visual aid, make sure you are in **control**. Be sure to **set your own pace** of delivery.

O If your script is hard to read in this format, **rewrite it.** Adjustments now will **pay off** later.

O Build in and script pauses to **sound natural.**

O Read ahead in **phrases** to look more natural.

O Deliberately **increase** your **blink rate** in order to prevent "teleprompter stare."

USING A PODIUM

Do's	Don'ts
O Placing papers high up on the podium to reduce "head bobbing" as you read	O Maintaining a "death grip" on the sides of the podium
O Sliding rather than turning pages to reduce noise and distraction	O Leaning on the podium
O Allowing the audience to respond; pausing to acknowledge applause or laughter if interrupted	O Tapping fingers on the podium or near the microphone
O Varying voice, tone, and pacing throughout the speech	O Allowing your voice to trail off at the ends of sentences
O Testing and adjusting podium height before beginning	O Turning your head away from a stationary microphone
O Standing squarely balanced on both feet at all times	O Fiddling with pens, paper clips, or anything else on the podium

Speaking from podiums

Speaker podiums give the presenter a place to stand, room to place a hard copy of the speech, and, sometimes, a stationary microphone. However, podiums can also pose problems. While they do provide some comfort, they may also create a physical barrier between speaker and audience that is a challenge to overcome. Even transparent podiums, designed to mitigate this problem, still force the speaker into a small, tightly constrained space, making it difficult for the audience to gauge their commitment and belief in what is being said.

Working the room

To counteract the constraints of a podium, exaggerate your gestures so you can be seen clearly. Use a handheld or lapel microphone to avoid obstructing

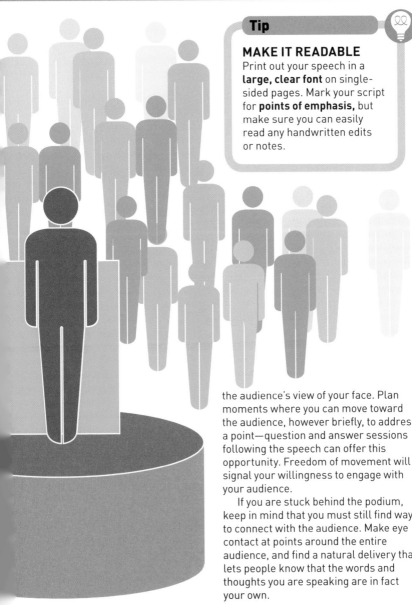

Tip

MAKE IT READABLE
Print out your speech in a
large, clear font on single-
sided pages. Mark your script
for **points of emphasis,** but
make sure you can easily
read any handwritten edits
or notes.

the audience's view of your face. Plan
moments where you can move toward
the audience, however briefly, to address
a point—question and answer sessions
following the speech can offer this
opportunity. Freedom of movement will
signal your willingness to engage with
your audience.

If you are stuck behind the podium,
keep in mind that you must still find ways
to connect with the audience. Make eye
contact at points around the entire
audience, and find a natural delivery that
lets people know that the words and
thoughts you are speaking are in fact
your own.

Running the Q&A

The question and answer part of your presentation is a great opportunity to drive home your key points and cement the bonds you have established with your audience. Q&A sessions keep an audience engaged and provide you with an invaluable insight into how they have received and understood your communication.

Making time for questions

Always allow time in every presentation for questions and answers or some other form of audience feedback. If your format doesn't allow for a session following your presentation, consider addressing questions as they come up.

Audiences often look forward to the question and answer session more than to the presentation itself. It is at this time that their needs move to center stage—they can engage with you directly and test the strength with which you hold your ideas. You should welcome the Q&A because the questions will indicate if you have been effective, and if you have addressed what the audience really wants to know. Consider the Q&A as feedback—a way of strengthening your presentation content and delivery.

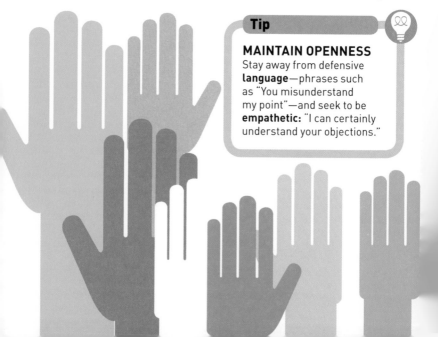

Tip

MAINTAIN OPENNESS
Stay away from defensive **language**—phrases such as "You misunderstand my point"—and seek to be **empathetic:** "I can certainly understand your objections."

In focus

WRAPPING UP

Signal in advance your intention to close off questions, with a statement such as, "We have time for two more questions and then I'll wrap this up." Don't just end abruptly after the last question is answered. Instead, take a moment to summarize your key points and offer your audience next steps or actions they can take. Be succinct in this final closing, and restate without repeating what has come before. Remember to leave on an upbeat and positive note, and thank people for their time and their attention.

Staying in control

Clearly signal the start of the Q&A session not only with your words but through body language; an open posture indicates you are ready for questions. Stay in control of the session at all times by directing the format and focus of the questions. Although this part of the presentation is unscripted, there are techniques to help keep the session focused:

- Keep questioners on track: if they begin to wander off the point, you could say, for example, "We're running short of time and I want to make sure we return to the immediate issue at hand."

Tip

USE TOUCHSTONES

Keep repeating **key words and phrases**—or touchstones— in your answers. This will **emphasize crucial points** and help audience retention.

Tip

GOOD QUESTION!

Don't overuse the **response:** "That's a good question!" or it will lose its meaning with your audience.

- Don't allow audience members to engage in their own separate debates, or to interrupt one another. Step in and direct the process with a quick assertion of control: "Susan, I'd like to hear your question, then we will turn to the issue Brian is raising."
- Seek to find common themes, or larger points that will get the discussion back to a message: "These are good points that deal with different ways to reach the goal we've been talking about."
- Don't dismiss questions even if it is clear that someone missed a key element of your presentation. Graciously repeat a quick summary for the questioner without making them feel awkward.

Answering tough questions

Even the best-prepared presenter will come up against hard questions, or difficult questioners. How you deal with these challenges can win or lose you the presentation, as the audience waits to see just how confidently and competently you can defend your position. In many cases, just staying calm and remaining in control under pressure is more important than having all the answers.

Anticipating situations

It is always easier to appear confident when you have done your research, so be prepared for your Q&A session. Although it is unscripted, you should be able to anticipate the questions you are most likely to be asked, and those you hope not to be asked. Be ready with suitable answers to both types, but also prepare to be surprised by unconventional

Tip

REPEAT THE QUESTION
In larger rooms, when wearing a microphone, **repeat or summarize** each question for the **benefit** of others in the audience before offering an answer.

questions. No one expects you to have all of the answers all of the time, so don't be afraid to say, "I don't know."

Maintaining poise

The key to handling difficult questions is keeping your poise. Maintain a calm demeanor, even if the questioner does not. Avoid signaling any discomfort through body language—stepping back from the audience or breaking eye contact, for example. If you have been standing up for the duration of the presentation, remain standing for the Q&A session.

Answering calmly

Keep a level tone, even if your answer is a candid "I don't know." If caught off guard by a question, buy some time; ask for the question to be repeated, or say that you will return to the question later. Even if your audience perceives the question as hostile or unfair, they will still want to see how you handle the response. Try not to take statements or questions personally, and address the answer to the entire audience while responding. Avoid being provoked and remember, you are in charge of your presentation.

Responding to questions

PROBLEM	SOLUTION	EXAMPLE
Long-winded or unfocused questions	**Pose the question differently**	"So what you're saying is there's been a lack of progress—is that right?"
	Ask for clarification	"I want to be sure I understand the question. Are you asking why we haven't made progress?"
Sceptical or hostile feedback	**Validate the concern**	"You're right about this approach carrying some risk, but we can mitigate that risk by the way we handle this."
	Empathize with the concern	"I understand your frustration. This has indeed been a long process. We'd all like to move forward now and get on with implementation."
	Stand firm	"I hear your concern, but let me respectfully disagree with your statement. Here's why."
Questions that stump	**Keep your cool**	"That's a good question. I don't have the answer for it. Here's what I can tell you though..."
	Return the question	"Let me ask you how you would answer that?" or "Can you clarify why you're asking that question?"
	Delay	"We can certainly discuss it after the session."

Dealing with the media

Media attention carries more credibility with audiences than advertising because it is perceived as being less partial and not paid for. It can help your organization to advance ideas or products, and build awareness and credibility with a targeted audience. However, not understanding media priorities can have severe negative consequences, even for smart businesses.

Understanding your role

Dealing effectively with independent media means recognizing the nature of the relationship that you are about to enter into. When you are interviewed, your role is not just to answer questions passively, it is to shape the agenda so that you can present your key messages succinctly and effectively. While you can't control the questions asked or the context, you do have control over access and over what you say. Maintaining a balance of control in interviews is a matter of delivering your messages well, through preparation and practice.

$16,250 (£10,000) was spent by UK government ministers on acting lessons from a drama school to improve their interviews and speeches

Shape the agenda so that you can present your key messages succinctly and effectively

Investing in training

Having expertise on a subject doesn't mean you are media-ready. In fact, being close to a topic often makes it difficult to speak in the broad and brief terms media interviews demand. Given that every media interview can impact on your organization's image and reputation, it is worth thinking about investing in training for all managers who are likely to come into contact with the media. Media training often provides managers with the best possible means to prepare for interviews. Training also helps managers to shape a story through their careful responses to the reporter's questions, and to meet the organization's requirements and the demands of reporters at the same time.

Ground rules for media interaction

AN INTERVIEW IS A BUSINESS TRANSACTION

Set yourself **a goal** for each interview, then **accomplish** it as briefly and as **memorably** as you possibly can. Know when to stop talking.

EVERYTHING IS ON THE RECORD

Reporters will **assume** that you know this. Anything you say **can and will** be **quoted** or broadcast.

BE CONCISE AND CONSISTENT

Understand your own message, and its **context.** Be firm when communicating it to the reporter.

AN INTERVIEW IS NOT A CHAT WITH A FRIEND

Reporters are **focused** on getting **a story**. They do not work for you and will **report** a story whether it serves your interests or not.

Talking to reporters

Anyone in business is a potential interview subject for a reporter searching for an expert opinion. Whether it is TV, radio, or print media, that opportunity, provided you get it right, can win you a wider platform to gain attention for a product or service, or to raise your own profile.

Preparing for the interview

Reporters are always under pressure to produce their stories. You will need to respect their deadlines while allowing yourself time to prepare thoroughly for an interview. Before the interview takes place, ask the reporter for the following information:

- What was it that captured their interest?
- What do they think that you can add to the story?
- What approach is being used—do they want a personal story, or a balancing opinion?
- What other sources will they be using—what can you uniquely add?
- Who is their primary audience?

Tip

FORM CONNECTIONS
Let the **reporter** know if there are others you are aware of who can provide information or **points of view** that can **aid** in understanding. Help the reporter get in touch with those resources.

Keeping it in context

Speaking to reporters under such circumstances—especially about controversial or news-based subjects— makes many people worry that they will be taken out of context. You can reduce the likelihood of this happening by planning ahead:

- Work your messages into a short, memorable form—sound bites for broadcast and quotes for print media. These are what you want the reporter to take away with them.
- Formulate "bridges"—ways of moving between an answer to an anticipated question and a sound bite that you have prepared.
- Seize the initiative by talking to the reporter about the subject, even before the questions begin. This is your opportunity to influence the direction of the interview.

Tip

MAKE INDEPENDENT STATEMENTS
Make sure everything you say to a reporter can **"stand alone"**; that is, make sure your statements are not entirely dependent on a specific context to be **understood correctly.**

BEING INTERVIEWED

Do's	Don'ts
O **Setting a clear goal for every interview**	O Assuming the reporter will explain your points for you
O **Taking the initiative in getting your points across**	O Hoping the reporter asks the right questions
O **Keeping answers short and memorable**	O Giving detailed responses and letting the reporter select the relevant parts
O **Staying focused on your messages and speaking about what you know**	O Guessing at a correct response or the views of others
O **Keeping your voice natural and lively**	O Speaking in a monotone
O **Anticipating the obvious questions as well as the toughest**	O Winging your way through and hoping for an easy ride
O **Correcting any inaccurate assumptions posed within questions**	O Letting inaccuracies stand

Getting your message across

A standard line of questioning for reporters concerns the "worst case scenario." Reporters who are seeking interesting comments are prone to press subjects to speculate on what might happen in a given case that the public might need to know. However, speculation—no matter how carefully phrased—is likely to create problems if you are quoted out of context. Replace speculation with an interesting comment about what you do know. You will be in a good position to do that if you understand what the reporter wants and develop your own well crafted messages to provide it.

Index